The Beach
That Love Built

Written by Russ Towne

Illustrated by Christina Cartwright

The Beach That Love Built
© 2016 Russ Towne
The Beach That Love Built
First Edition, May 2016

Russ Towne Publishing
Campbell, CA

Editing: Shayla Eaton, CuriouserEditing.com
Layout and Cover Design: Gail Nelson, e-book-design.com
Illustrations: Christina Cartwright

ISBN-13: 978-0-692-74214-3
ISBN-10: 0-692-74214-3

To Stephy:

May your life be a long, healthy, and happy adventure!

This is a true story about a
young girl named Stephy.

One day, Stephy got very sick and had to stay in the hospital for a long, long time. This made her and everyone who loved her very sad.

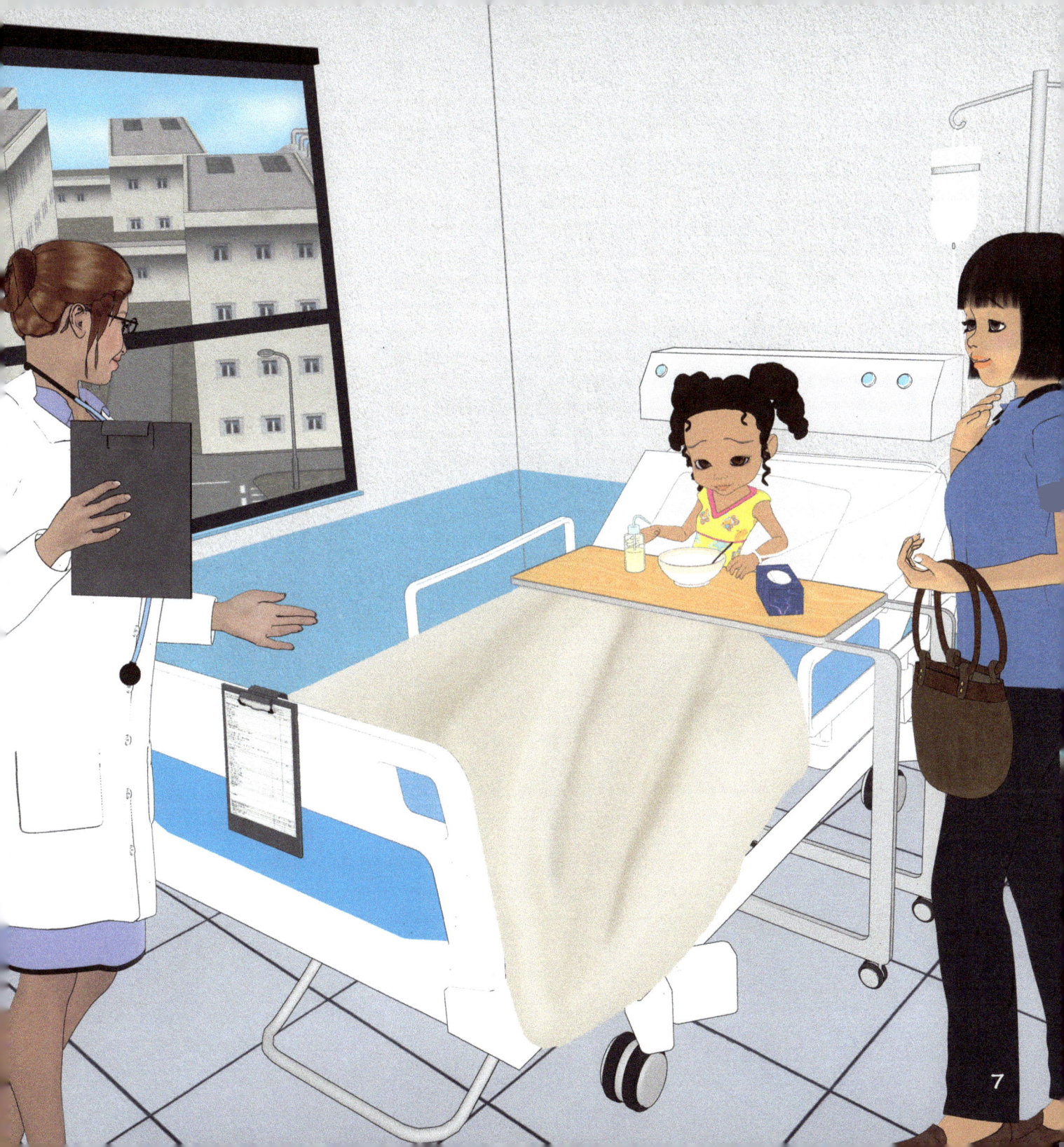

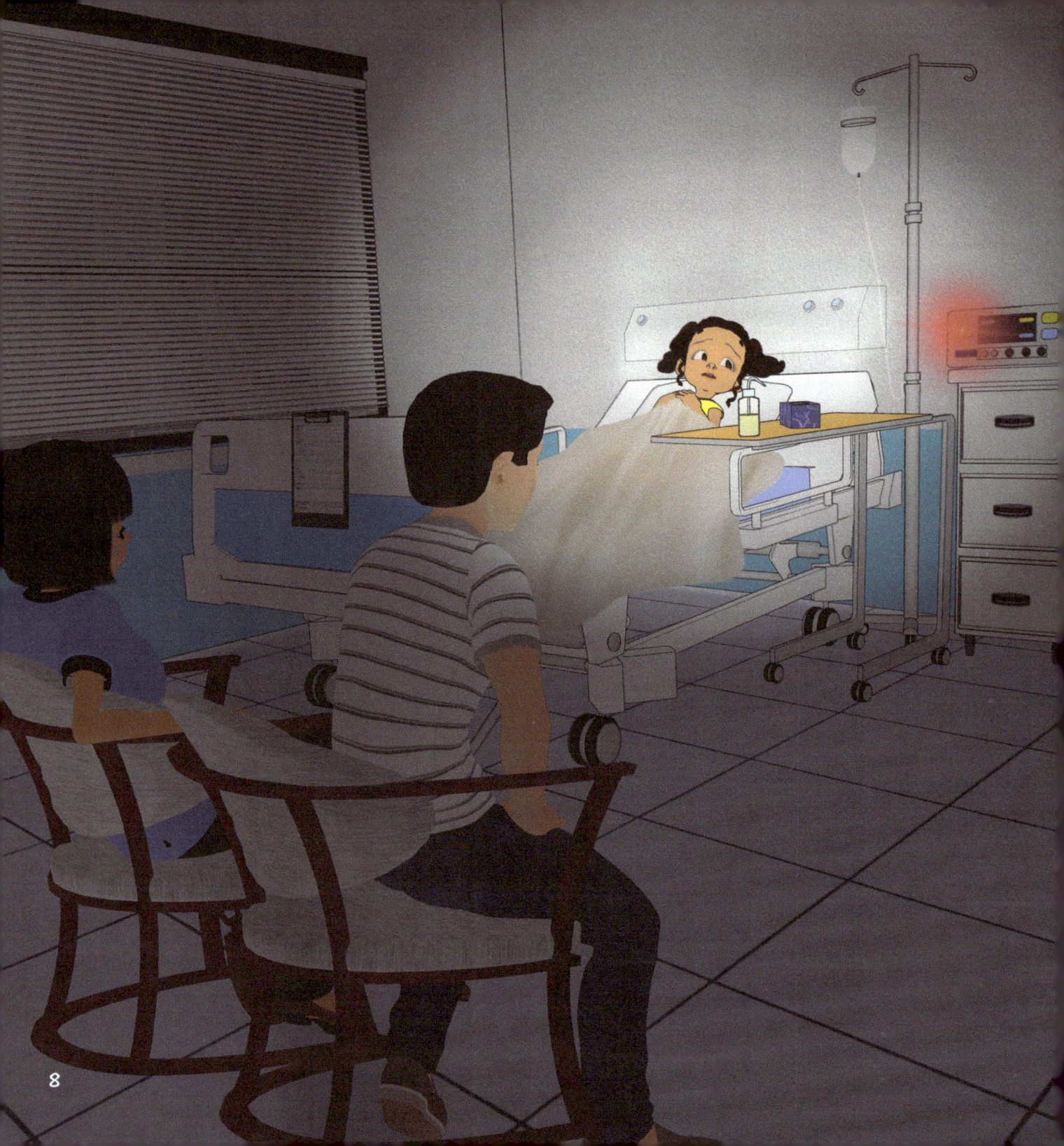

Her mommy and daddy were always there. They even slept in a chair next to her at night. Everyone at the hospital was friendly, and they all took great care of her. But Stephy didn't like having so many strangers around her all the time. And some of the noises from the machines startled her when she slept.

She wanted to leave but the doctors said she was not well enough yet. Stephy was tired of being so sick and she wanted to go home. She missed playing with her puppy named Ginger, her brothers, and her friends at school.

11

Finally, the doctor said Stephy was well enough to go home! Everyone was so happy. When Stephy walked through the front door of their house, Ginger ran up to her with her tail swoosh-swooshing. Stephy knelt down and gave Ginger a great big hug as Ginger licked all over her face.

It would soon be Stephy's birthday, so her mommy and daddy asked her what she would like. She said, "When I was in the hospital, I dreamed of having a day at the beach with Ginger, our family, and my friends, and then a bonfire that night."

Her mommy and daddy wanted to make this birthday extra-special and went to work planning her party. They found that only one beach in the area allowed dogs and bonfires and was easy to get to for her grandparents so that's where they planned to go.

Stephy was so excited that she asked her mommy every day if today was the day.

The night before the party, Daddy's friend Ian called and said, "I have some very bad news. We can't use that beach tomorrow after all. Two cities are using it for other things. I tried to find other beaches that allow puppies and bonfires and were easy to get to, but none are in the area."

When Daddy told Stephy the news, she sat down and quietly began to cry. She quickly decided she'd rather have the party at her house so she could at least have Ginger, her relatives, friends, and a bonfire.

Early the next morning, while Stephy was still sleeping, her mommy and daddy heard a knock on the door. It was her daddy's friend, Ian. He said, "I knew how sad Stephy was when she couldn't go to the beach so I decided to bring the beach to her."

He pointed to his car. So much sand was in the trunk that it looked like it was about to scrape the ground. The backseat was filled with all kinds of things. Tiki torches and a palm tree with lights poked out of the back windows.

Everyone quietly got right to work while Stephy slept.

When guests arrived, they were surprised to find a sign that read:

Welcome to Stephy's Beach, where puppies and bonfires are welcome. Where the beach is small and the waves are so far away that you need to close your eyes to see them, but it's easy to see our love for Stephy and her little dog too!

Happy Birthday, Stephy!

Then they saw the goofiest beach they'd ever seen. The sand was spread out around a wading pool. Beach toys and seashells were scattered all around. A small palm tree waved in the breeze near fish nets hung on a wall. Tiki torches stood all around.

The beach had been built with so much love that it magically became real to everyone. Stephy and her friends made sand castles, covered each other with sand, played and splashed in the water, and laughed and laughed. They had a big barbecue, and then everyone got to make their own huge ice-cream sundaes, sing Happy Birthday, and eat birthday cake.

They watched a beautiful sunset. Then, as the moon rose and stars began to appear in the sky, the lights on the palm tree sparkled like fireflies. Flames from the tiki torches and a bonfire made everything warm and beautiful. In the darkness with the stars, twinkling lights, and glow from the fires, the scene magically became a beach at night.

Stephy looked around, smiled, and stopped playing with her friends. She walked over to her mommy and daddy and gave them a great big hug as she whispered, "Thank you for making my birthday dream come true! I love you."

About the Author

Russ lives with his wife in Campbell, California. They've been married since 1979 and have three children and three grandsons. In addition to enjoying his family and friends, and his dual passions for investing and writing, Russ loves to spend time in nature, especially near rivers and streams that run through giant redwood groves, and near beautiful beaches. He enjoys watching classic movies, reading, and tending to his small fern garden and redwood grove. Russ manages the investments of the wealth management firm he founded in 2003. He has published fifteen books, nine of which are children's books.

Russ's books can all be found on Amazon. His Amazon Author Page can be found at www.amazon.com/author/RussTowne.

Books for Young Children

Purple Fox and the Heebie Jeebies
Misty Zebracorn
Zach and the Toad Who Road a Bull
V. G. and Me
The Grumpadinkles
Ki-Gra's REALLY, REALLY BIG Day!
The Duck Who Flew Upside Down
Clyde and Friends Coloring Book
Clyde and Friends
Clyde and Hoozy Whatzadingle
Clyde and I Help a Hippo to Fly
Rusty Bear and Thomas Too
Clyde and I

Children's App

Based on Characters from his Clyde Books: Clyde and Friends
children's app developed by Gail Nelson using characters from
Russ's series of Clyde books: www.clydeandfriends.com.

Russ's Blog

Clyde and Friends — www.ClydeandFriends.com

Stay updated on Russ's latest children's books, apps, songs, and merchandise (featuring the animated characters that appear in his stories). Readers get sneak previews of special stories, background information about where his story ideas come from and how they are developed, and opportunities to help Russ prioritize the order in which his stories and books should be published, the look, and sometimes the names of some of his characters.

www.ingramcontent.com/pod-product-compliance
Lightning Source LLC
Chambersburg PA
CBHW040249100426
42811CB00011B/1206